Learn About

THE FIVE SENSES

Touching

by Sonia W. Black

Children's Press®
An imprint of Scholastic Inc.

Special thanks to our medical content consultant, An Huang, MD, PhD, professor of physiology, New York Medical College.

Library of Congress Cataloging-in-Publication Data
Names: Black, Sonia W., 1953– author.
Title: Touching / by Sonia W. Black.
Description: First edition. | New York, NY: Children's Press, an imprint of Scholastic Inc., 2024. | Series: Learn about: the five senses | Includes bibliographical references and index. | Audience: Ages 5–7. | Audience: Grades K–1. | Summary: "How do we experience the world? Let's learn all about the five senses! The sense of touch is one of our five senses. And it is amazing! Every day it starts working the very same moment we wake. It tells us that our pillow feels soft, the floor is hard, the shower is hot, and the juice is cold. Touch also tells us that tickling feels good and bumping into something feels bad. Learn about feeling, how it works, and common problems and diseases connected with it with this perfect first introduction to the sense of touch! ABOUT THE SERIES: The human body is amazing! It gives us five different ways to learn about the world around us: through the eyes, through the skin, through the tongue, through the ears, and through the nose. Thanks to these parts of our bodies, we can see, feel, taste, hear, and smell. These are the five senses! Why do bananas taste so good? Why does tickling cause so much laughter? Illustrated with familiar examples, this fun nonfiction set in the Learn About series gives readers a close-up look at the five senses, and it teaches them how each of the senses work."— Provided by publisher.
Identifiers: LCCN 2022056762 (print) | LCCN 2022056763 (ebook) | ISBN 9781338898170 (library binding) | ISBN 9781338898187 (paperback) | ISBN 9781338898194 (ebk)
Subjects: LCSH: Touch—Juvenile literature. | Skin—Juvenile literature. | Senses and sensation—Juvenile literature. | BISAC: JUVENILE NONFICTION / Concepts / Senses & Sensation | JUVENILE NONFICTION / General
Classification: LCC QP451 .B63 2024 (print) | LCC QP451 (ebook) | DDC 612.8/8—dc23/eng/20230124
LC record available at https://lccn.loc.gov/2022056762
LC ebook record available at https://lccn.loc.gov/2022056763

Copyright © 2024 by Scholastic Inc.

All rights reserved. Published by Children's Press, an imprint of Scholastic Inc., *Publishers since 1920.* SCHOLASTIC, CHILDREN'S PRESS, and associated logos are trademarks and/or registered trademarks of Scholastic Inc.

The publisher does not have any control over and does not assume any responsibility for author or third-party websites or their content.

No part of this publication may be reproduced, stored in a retrieval system, or transmitted in any form or by any means, electronic, mechanical, photocopying, recording, or otherwise, without written permission of the publisher. For information regarding permission, write to Scholastic Inc., Attention: Permissions Department, 557 Broadway, New York, NY 10012.

10 9 8 7 6 5 4 3 2 1   24 25 26 27 28

Printed in China, 62
First edition, 2024

Book design by Kathleen Petelinsek

Photos ©: cover, 1: Richard T. Nowitz/Getty Images; 4–5: Steve Satushek/Getty Images; 6 left: moodboard/Getty Images; 6 center: g&l images/Getty Images; 7 left: 478217355, JodiJacobson/Getty Images; 7 center: Stefania Pelfini, La Waziya Photography/Getty Images; 7 right: Sally Anscombe/Getty Images; 8: SolStock/Getty Images; 10 right: JGI/Jamie Grill/Getty Images; 11 right: Antonio_Diaz/Getty Images; 12–13: 7activestudio/Getty Images; 21 top: Kwangmoozaa/Getty Images; 21 bottom: Evgen_Prozhyrko/Getty Images; 22: Sally Anscombe/Getty Images; 24: FamVeld/Getty Images; 26 bottom right: chengyuzheng/Getty Images; 28 top: benedek/Getty Images; 28 center: Tom Soucek/Design Pics Inc/Alamy Images; 28 bottom: FLPA/Shutterstock; 29 top: Jenhung Huang/Getty Images; 29 center: LionH/Getty Images; 29 bottom: Paul Gilham/Getty Images; 30 top left: yaruta/Getty Images; 30 top right: Copyright Crezalyn Nerona Uratsuji/Getty Images; 30 center right: RonTech2000/Getty Images; 30 bottom right: ImagineGolf/Getty Images.

All other photos © Shutterstock.

TABLE OF CONTENTS

Touching and Feeling......................4

Chapter 1: Amazing Touch................6

Chapter 2: How Touch Works...........12

Chapter 3: Problems with Our Skin and Touch............................18

Activity: Touch and Tell....................26

Animal Touch................................28

Protect Your Sense of Touch!...30

Glossary..31

Index/About the Author...........32

INTRODUCTION

Touching and Feeling

It's fun to pet animals at a petting zoo. The baby chicks and bunnies feel so soft and fluffy. What makes us able to feel? It's our sense of touch.

Touch is one of our five senses. The other four are hearing, sight, smell, and taste. Our senses give us information about the world around us. Touch tells us how *everything* feels.

We experience touch with our *whole* body.

CHAPTER 1

Amazing Touch

We use our sense of touch from the moment we wake. Touch makes us feel all kinds of **textures**, shapes, and sensations.

Our pillows feel soft. The floor feels hard. The toast is hot. The juice is cold. The toothbrush is thin. We paint wet watercolor onto dry paper. We hang our paintings with sharp thumbtacks.

You can't turn off your sense of touch.

The feeling of getting tickled is pressure. It makes you laugh. But, did you know you can't tickle yourself?

Our sense of touch makes us feel pressure. That's the feeling you get from a handshake or a warm hug. That pressure feels good.

But, if you get grabbed and tackled, that pressure is hard. That does not feel pleasant. Touch causes us to feel pain, too. For example, you can feel pain if you bump into something. This happens to protect us. Feeling pain tells us something is wrong.

Hot sand is painful on your bare feet. Your sense of touch is warning, "Get off the sand!"

Today, we live in a world filled with technology. Just think about some things you do. Thanks to our sense of touch, we get to use all kinds of electronics.

With a tap of our fingers, we can play fun video games, and work computers and tablets. We can even use a cell phone.

We need our sense of touch to use technology.

CHAPTER 2

How Touch Works

Skin plays a big role in how our sense of touch works. Did you know the skin is the largest **organ** in our body? It covers us from head to toe!

EPIDERMIS: This is the thin, outer layer of skin. We get our skin color from **melanin** in this layer. This layer keeps harmful **germs** from entering our bodies.

The epidermis has keratin. It helps your hair grow healthy and strong.

Hair

Receptor

12

Look at your face and hands. You see only the top layer of skin. But our skin has three different layers.

Our dermis has over 4 million receptors.

DERMIS: This layer has elastic threads called fibers. These fibers let our skin stretch. **Receptors** in this layer make us feel heat, cold, pain, and pressure.

SUBCUTIS, OR HYPODERMIS: This layer is full of fat cells. Fat works like padding for our body. It protects our bones and muscles from bumps and falls. And it maintains our body temperature.

13

Our receptors and nerves work together with our brain to let us feel different types of touch. Here's what happens when you touch something. Receptors send a message through your nerves, up your spinal cord, and to the brain. The brain checks the message. Right away, it lets you know things like, "That's itchy," "That feels soft," "That's hard," or "Stop! That hurts!"

The spinal cord is a long bundle of nerves. It runs from the brain down the back.

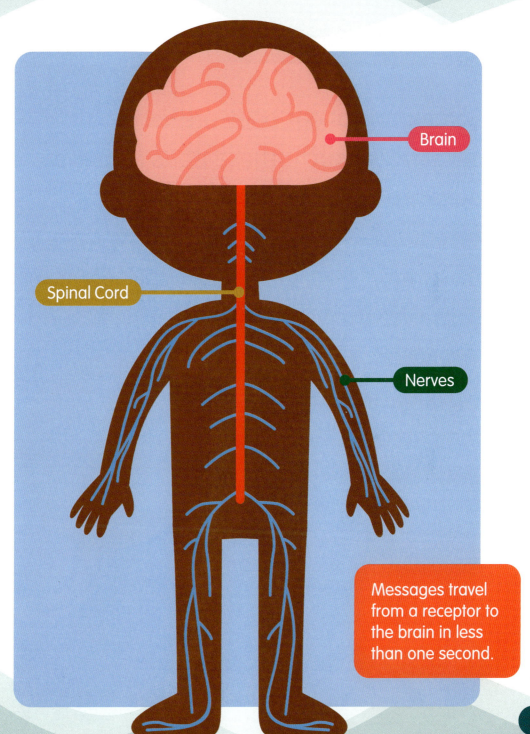

Some parts of our body are very sensitive to touch. These parts respond quickly because they have a lot of touch receptors. Other parts of our body have fewer touch receptors. They are not as sensitive. They may be slower to respond. What body parts fall into which group? Look at the photo on the next page and see.

Each fingertip has more than 3,000 touch receptors.

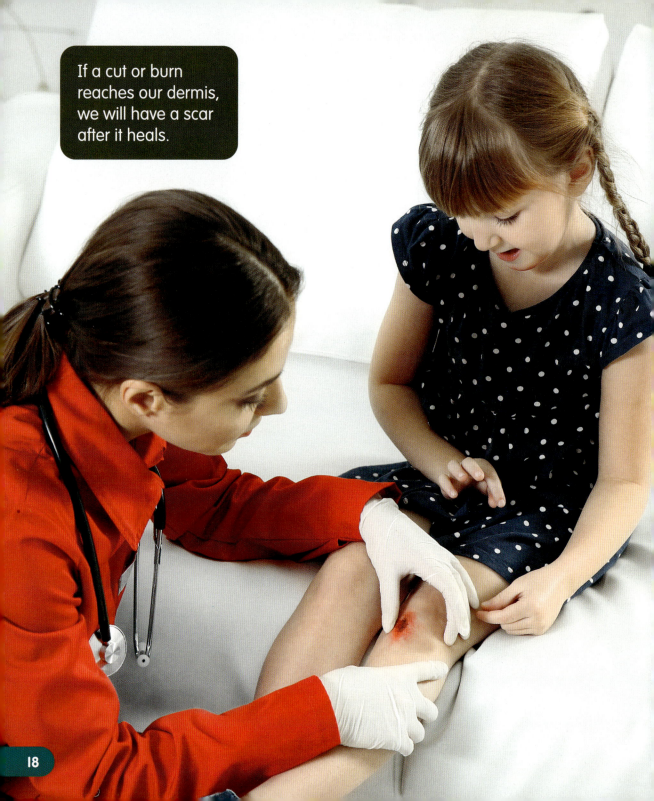

If a cut or burn reaches our dermis, we will have a scar after it heals.

CHAPTER 3

Problems with Our Skin and Touch

Sometimes we may fall and bump into things. We can get cuts, scrapes, or bruises. We can also get a burn if we touch something hot. An open wound may appear on the skin. We need to disinfect, or clean, open wounds. After that, we might want to apply an **antibiotic** cream. A wound can be covered with a bandage or gauze. This helps to prevent germs from causing an **infection**.

Some insects, like mosquitoes, bedbugs, and bees, can bite or sting our skin. A red bump can appear. It may be itchy and painful!

Only female mosquitoes bite. When they do, they shoot a liquid into your skin. This causes the bumps and itching.

Our skin can also get a rash. The skin is **irritated**. It gets bumpy and itchy. Many things, such as heat and allergies, can cause a rash. A doctor can help us treat it.

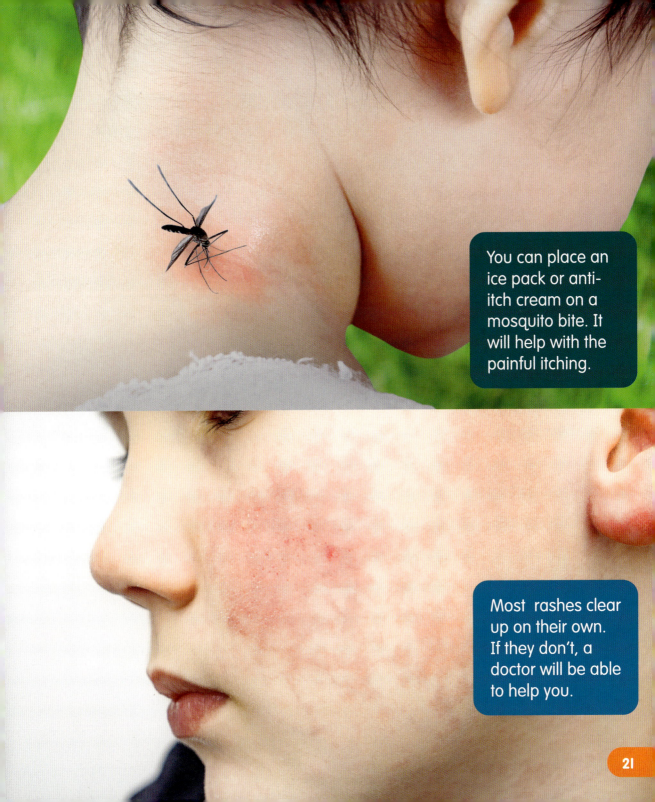

You can place an ice pack or anti-itch cream on a mosquito bite. It will help with the painful itching.

Most rashes clear up on their own. If they don't, a doctor will be able to help you.

Sunburn happens when skin is exposed to too much sun.

Sunburn makes the skin feel very hot. Skin gets red, painful, and sensitive to the touch. What helps? Cool, wet towels and special creams can help soothe the burn.

A fever makes our skin feel hot, too! A doctor can give us medicine to help us bring down the temperature of the skin.

Fingers, toes, ears, cheeks, chin, and nose are the parts of our body that are more likely to freeze with frostbite.

Frostbite makes body parts freeze from being too cold. It is painful! Frostbite can happen if you stay outdoors in very cold temperatures for a very long time. What helps? Get indoors so your body can get warm again.

Touch receptors in our feet help us to stand.

As we get older, our bodies slowly lose some touch receptors. So, our sense of touch becomes less and less sensitive over time. That is why elderly people fall sometimes. They have lost a lot of the touch receptors from the bottom of their feet.

The sense of touch is truly amazing. Together with the other senses, it keeps us connected to the world around us. What will your senses help you do today?

> Some people do not have a sense of touch. They can't feel anything at all. It is very rare.

ACTIVITY: TOUCH AND TELL

Use only your sense of touch to name different textures and shapes. You can do this activity with one or more people.

YOU WILL NEED:

- A blindfold
- 3 or 4 shoeboxes
- Pairs of household items with different textures and shapes. Dice, round buttons, cotton balls, sandpaper, apples, seashells, toothbrushes, and sponges are good choices.
- An adult to help

STEPS:

1. Have an adult cut a big hole on the lid of each shoebox.
2. Place one of each matching item in a different box.
3. Blindfold the participants.
4. Have participants take turns to select a box. Have them place a hand inside the box and remove one item. They must describe its texture and/or shape. Then, while still blindfolded, have them find the matching item from any of the other boxes.

WHAT HAPPENED?

Your sense of touch becomes more sensitive when you're blindfolded. This means you pay closer attention. This helps you identify textures and shapes and tell what the items are.

ANIMAL TOUCH

Rough, Tough Skin

Alligators and crocodiles have very tough skin. It is spiky. It has hard, bony scales underneath. It is super sensitive to touch. The skin can feel **vibrations** in the water from faraway ripples. Some vibrations alert these animals that a meal is near.

Powerful Paws

A sea otter's paws are really sensitive to touch. The sea otter swims along the ocean floor looking for food. It is very dark there. But the otter's paws can feel a clam and—quick as a wink—grab it for dinner.

Funny Nose

The star-nosed mole has star-shaped, pointy pink skin around its nose. The mole lives mostly underground. Its funny-looking nose has touch sensors. These help the mole to feel its way around in the dark underground.

Warning Whiskers

A manatee has around 2,000 whiskers. They help the manatee find food. The sensitive whiskers feel vibrations in the water. The vibrations tell the manatee if another animal is around.

Hairy Legs

Spiders have eight legs. These legs are covered with an amazing number of hairs. The hairs feel even the tiniest vibrations. Often, the vibrations are caused by future food stuck in the spider's web. The spider can then quickly find it and snatch it for a yummy meal!

Big Thick Feet

Elephants are some of the largest animals in the world. The thick skin on the bottom of their huge feet can feel vibrations coming from far away. This helps them keep safe. The vibrations could warn of enemy animals, such as lions or hyenas, approaching.

PROTECT YOUR SENSE OF TOUCH!

If you protect your skin, you are protecting your sense of touch. You can do this in different ways.

You can cover your head with a cap or hat on hot and especially sunny days. You can also use sunscreen.

Raincoats, rain boots, and umbrellas will keep you dry in rainy weather.

Don't get too close to a fire to avoid getting burned.

A coat or jacket, hat, scarf, gloves, and boots will keep you warm on cold winter days.

Make sure you wear protective gear when you play sports. It helps you prevent scrapes and bruises.

GLOSSARY

antibiotic (an-ti-bye-AH-tik) a drug that kills bacteria and is used to treat infections and diseases

germs (JURMZ) tiny living organisms that can cause disease

infection (in-FEK-shuhn) an illness caused by bacteria or viruses

irritated (IR-i-tate-id) sore or sensitive

melanin (ME-luh-nuhn) a dark-brown pigment present in skin, hair, and other tissues that helps to determine the color of the skin, hair, and eyes

organ (OR-guhn) a part of the body, such as the skin or the heart, that has a certain purpose

receptors (ri-SEP-turz) nerve endings that sense stimulus, such as pressure, touch, or heat

textures (TEKS-churz) the way some things feel, especially how rough or smooth they are

vibrations (vye-BRAY-shuhnz) rapid movements that go back and forth

INDEX

animals, 28–29
antibiotics, 19
fever, 22
frostbite, 23
germs, 12
infection, 19
insect bites, 20–21
irritated skin, 20–21
keratin, 12
melanin, 12
nerves, 14–15

organs, 12
pain, 9
pressure, 8–9
rashes, 20–21
receptors, 13, 14–16, 24–25
scars, 18
sensitivity, 16–17
shapes, feeling, 6–7, 26–27

skin
  parts of, 12–17
  problems with, 18–25
  protecting, 30
sunburn, 22
technology, 10–11
textures, 6–7, 26–27
tickling, 8
touch problems, 18–25
vibrations, 28–29

ABOUT THE AUTHOR

Writing this book stirred up a favorite childhood memory for **Sonia W. Black**. The author of numerous children's books, Ms. Black remembers helping her great-grandmother Mammie look after the baby chicks Mammie raised. She vividly recalls the warmest, softest feel of the newborn chicks' fluffy yellow feathers. Nowadays, Ms. Black enjoys cuddling and petting her furry dog, Lucky.